KNOW ALL ABOUT TACK

George Dulaney

Bill Weikel, Editor
THE FARNAM HORSE LIBRARY

HORSE LIBRARY

The Farnam Horse Library
8701 North 29th Street
Omaha, Nebraska 68112

CONTENTS

KNOW ALL ABOUT TACK

There is little doubt that questions exist in the minds of many horsemen concerning the wide variety of saddles, bridles, bits, martingales, girths, boots, plus all of the incidental items which make up a seemingly unending variety of horse *tack*. What is it? Where did it originate? How is it made? What is its purpose? The questions seem endless as horsemen everywhere seek solutions to training problems and riding efficiency.

Saddles must not only be comfortable to both horse and rider, they must also fit the uses to which they are put. Thus the stock horse saddle is a vastly different item than is the light-weight jockey saddle of today's racing world. Bits, bridles, spurs, etc., can be categorized as communication devices. The more you understand *how* they work, the more expert your horsemanship will become. ■

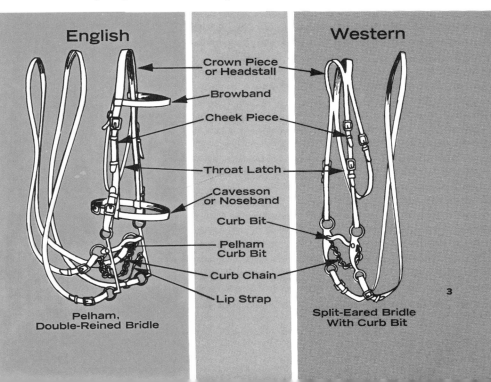

English

Western

Crown Piece or Headstall

Browband

Cheek Piece

Throat Latch

Cavesson or Noseband

Curb Bit

Pelham Curb Bit

Curb Chain

Lip Strap

Pelham,
Double-Reined Bridle

Split-Eared Bridle
With Curb Bit

3

English

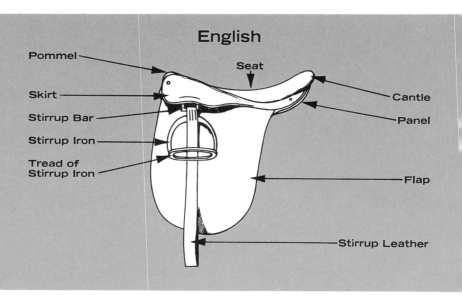

Pommel

Seat

Skirt

Cantle

Stirrup Bar

Panel

Stirrup Iron

Tread of
Stirrup Iron

Flap

Stirrup Leather

Western

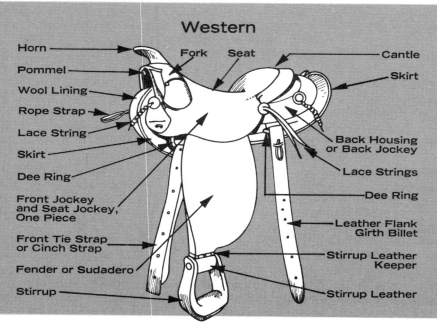

Horn

Fork   Seat

Cantle

Pommel

Skirt

Wool Lining

Rope Strap

Lace String

Back Housing
or Back Jockey

Skirt

Lace Strings

Dee Ring

Dee Ring

Front Jockey
and Seat Jockey,
One Piece

Leather Flank
Girth Billet

Front Tie Strap
or Cinch Strap

Stirrup Leather
Keeper

Fender or Sudadero

Stirrup

Stirrup Leather

4

CHAPTER ONE

WHERE DID THEY ORIGINATE?

Historians tell us that horses were domesticated as riding and draft animals as early as 2150 B.C. in what could now be geographically considered Scandinavia.* There is also evidence that civilized people of China, India, and Mesopotamia were using horses as a means of transportation during this same period in history. The first known galloping race with mounted rider was run in the thirty-third Olympiad in 645 B.C.

These early horsemen developed the ancient forms of the saddle plus rudimentary control devices as they came to perceive the advantages which would accrue from doing so. Stirrups and a more secure seat enabled man to wield a sword or spear from horseback, rather than having to dismount in order to partake of these activities. Improved control of their mounts made superior horsemen of those who experimented with early forms of the bit, and this in turn made them formidable foes on the battlefield. From these early necessities came the tremendous variety and sophistication of our modern saddles and all other forms of horse equipment which provide not only a precise control but also add a degree of comfort for both rider and animal unknown to the early rider.

Public and private collections in evidence all over the world present many well-preserved articles of horse gear and some items date back over one thousand years. There are samples of saddlery from many different parts of the world which bear a marked similarity even though the people involved probably had no contact with each other. This supports the theory that the origin of horsemanship was not confined to any one particular race or country.

Many of the early saddles show a resemblance to saddles used today and much research leads to the author's opinion that there is no *true type* in any of the various styles of saddlery. All modern saddles have copied some part of their design from saddles that originated in the Far East, areas of North Africa or the mountains and plains of Northern Europe.

Historians have concluded that saddles, as such, must have originated in the Orient and were introduced by the hordes of Ghengis

*Editor's note — There will be a certain amount of disagreement among horsemen regarding where and when horses were first domesticated. Wherever and whenever it happened, we are grateful to those who participated.

Khan, Attila the Hun, and Tammerlane who, in different periods of history, overran what is now Continental Europe. While these golden hordes absorbed much of the customs and cultures of their subjected and beaten peoples, they also left behind many of their customs and artifacts among which there was much horse knowledge and gear.

The saddle, using the term in a broad sense, is not confined for use exclusively on a horse. There are saddles used and designed for other ridable animals. The camel saddle in its simple form is nothing more than an X-shaped frame, front and back, with a kind of platform joining both tree bows. A leather or cloth cushion is placed on this platform between the bows and secured in place. Depending of course on personal taste and wealth, some of these saddles are very ornate and are built very high in the pommel and cantle with richly decorated tapestries, colored leathers, and precious metals.

Many of the horse saddles used by the early Spanish show an influence of design similar to the more elaborate type of camel saddle, including the high pommel and cantle with all their trappings and decoration. This influence is probably due to the Moorish occupation of Spain, as attested to by the Moorish influence in their art, their buildings and especially their leather work. The curb bit so dear to the Spanish horsemen was introduced to Spain by the Moors.

The Howdah, or affair which is used on the back of an elephant that resembles a small house, essentially is a saddle of sorts. Also there are the crude saddles of wood and sometimes leather which are used on the backs of water buffalo and oxen. So, we see that the saddle is primarily a seat contoured to fit various kinds of animals as well as their riders to give control and comfort to all; it is not an appliance strictly for the horse.

The hordes of Mongols, Huns, and other Northern tribes that overran Europe from time to time, probably contributed a great variety of saddlery to Europe. These nomads who lived on horseback were superb horsemen from necessity, and each tribe had horse gear that was designed for performance and comfort. It has been said that these horsemen placed a slab of raw meat under their saddles as a pad, and that this was later eaten on their long marches. It would be hard to find a better cushion between a saddle and a horse's back. These horsemen rode exclusively with a type of snaffle bit and a very short stirrup. This gave their wiry horses great galloping freedom and their riders a lot of mobility to use their weapons effectively when attacking.

The influence of the Spanish on the design of saddlery has been

Historians conclude that saddles must have originated in the Orient. This early (1570) Italian saddle displays an "Eastern" influence supporting the theory.

very important in the evolution of our stock saddle as we know it today. When the Conquistadores opened South America, Mexico, and parts of our Southern States, they were followed later by Spanish colonists who brought with them cattle, horses, and mules. These settlers were basically stockmen, and as their herds grew and ranged over larger areas of unfenced country, it became increasingly more important to have some supervision over these roving bands of cattle and horses. Thus the vaquero or cowboy was born. Spending long hours in the saddle, he from time to time added useful attachments to help him in his work. Riding in rough, brushy country, he added a leather hood over his stirrup, a *tapadero*. When it became necessary to rope or otherwise subdue an unruly cow or bull, then drag him out of the brush, he added a usable post to *dally* (anchor) his *riate* (rope). Thus the saddle horn was born. It is evident that the saddle horn is not original to this country inasmuch as saddles discovered in Poland as early as 1664 show a definite horn very similar to the charro type horn used by the vaquero.

As these inventions or innovations were copied from ranch to

7

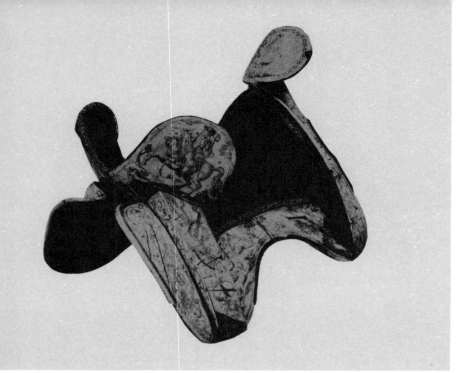

It is evident that the saddle horn is not original to this country inasmuch as saddles originating in Poland as early as 1664 show a definite horn very similar to the charro type used by the vaquero.

ranch and as they gradually proved their worth, new saddles were built incorporating many of these features. Then as ranchmen with their cattle ranged farther north and west, the Mexican influence weakened, giving way to rigging (method of keeping the saddle in place on the horse's back) designed to suit the changing terrain. In some sections of the country, the double rig was the most popular. The midwestern farmer used the popular center fire, single rig from a mail order house.

As time moved on, specific saddles were designed for specific jobs, such as a slick fork for roping or a swelled cut under fork for the cutting horse. Today there are as many types of saddles in the stock saddle range as there are personal tastes. Many of these saddles have tremendous eye appeal but have very little else to recommend them as much of the new look in stock saddles is only "for pretty" (to quote the Amish) and does not contribute anything to its comfort or wearing qualities. ■

CHAPTER TWO

MILITARY SADDLES

The McClellen Saddle

From a standpoint of utility and rugged service, there has never been a saddle to compare with the McClellen. This saddle was the standard of the U.S. Military from the time of the War between the States all the way up to World War II; it was used by mounted men in every branch of the service. The Horse Marines used it in China, and the Coast Guard used it in beach patrol work in World War II. It was the universal saddle of the mounted U.S. Military.

The McClellen was beautiful in its simplicity. It had no padding of any type; a folded blanket was used between the saddle and the horse. It was essentially a tree covered with leather stretched tight and stitched around the edges. The rigging was center fire, and secured at the pommel and cantle with brass screws, the cinch was braided horsehair. Some styles had hooded stirrups while some had iron English type stirrups. Approaching World War II, the Quartermaster Department modified some of these saddles by adding a flap cut on the same pattern as the English saddle. They also added billet straps sewn to webbing which was secured under the flap to the tree. This was done to permit the use of a leather girth in place of the horsehair cinch. It is interesting to note that saddles from Korea and Tibet dated during the fifteenth and sixteenth century A.D. are very similar to the McClellen saddle.

The Phillips Pattern Saddle

The United States Army Equitation School at Fort Riley, Kansas — when it was in operation — stressed what is known as a *balanced seat* on a horse. This meant neither behind the horse's action nor ahead of it. The theory was in balance at all times while walking, galloping, trotting, jumping, over any terrain, and under all conditions.

The Phillips Pattern saddle developed at that time was a combination of the hunting type English saddle, with some of the features of the French officer's saddle, but was designed to put the rider in a balanced position. These saddles were beautifully designed and built

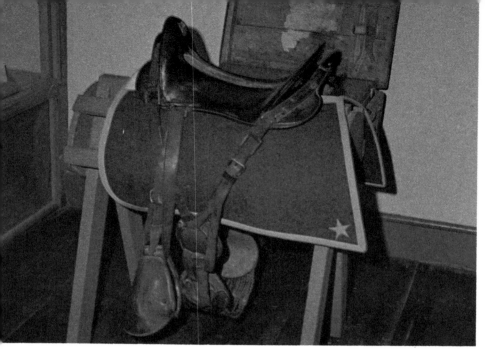

The McClellen saddle was beautiful in its simplicity. It had no padding of any type. A folded blanket was used between the saddle and the horse.

to stand up under rugged use. The overall appearance was similar to a modified forward seat saddle as we know it. A few years ago a number of these saddles were offered by one of the saddlery mail order houses and were sold out quickly. It is certain that there are many of these in use throughout the country today.

The Officer's Field Saddle

This saddle was patterned after the usual flat or hunting type saddle, except that it was much heavier and built for more rugged use. A feature of this design was to distribute the rider's weight over a greater area of the horse's back and this was accomplished by extending the bars of the tree about six inches past the cantle of the saddle and, of course, carrying the panel to the end of the tree points.

This pattern of saddle is still being offered by most saddlery houses under the name semi-military saddle. It has been modified somewhat, but it is an excellent saddle for a heavy rider who spends long hours in the saddle. It is also an excellent saddle for competitive trail rides as it will fit almost any horse. Due to the extended panel, this saddle is more suited to a long back rather than a short back. ■

CHAPTER THREE

STOCK SADDLES

Origin Of The Stock Saddle

As noted earlier, the stock or working saddle migrated from below the border in old Mexico into Texas, then spread west and north as the Indians were pushed back and cattle migrated into what had been buffalo country. Apparently when the Mexican style saddle reached Texas, the Texan changed the rigging. The Mexican saddle with its Spanish influence was single-rigged almost straight down from the root of the horn. The Texas style of rigging added another ring just below the root of the cantle. This became the full double rig. The flat, wide horn was discarded for a more upright round top horn that had a half-apple shape.

As the Texan changed the Spanish type saddle to suit his own purpose, the cattlemen of California also added their contribution. The rigging was moved back to a location just below the lowest point of the seat, this became the center fire rig. The Californian also added a taller, thinner, more graceful horn, and rounded the skirts which gave the saddle a more finished and pleasing look. These early changes in rigging were apparently caused by necessity rather than being merely a matter of taste. Saddles were rigged to fit the type horses used in different areas. Many of the problems encountered today in saddling are a result of a rider buying a saddle because he likes the style of rigging without taking into consideration the conformation of his horse.

It should be remembered that the development of the saddle stems from saddles used by the nomads of Eastern Europe. These people were herdsmen, and all of their equipment was purely functional. In all of our modern saddles, we can see the same basic design that originated possibly two thousand or more years ago.

The Modern Stock Saddle

With the emphasis on pleasure riding, much has been added to the modern stock saddle — quilted, padded overlays on the seat, elaborate tooling and embossing, the use of stainless steel and silver ornaments, plus thonging or as it is known today, buckstitching. Then too, rigging

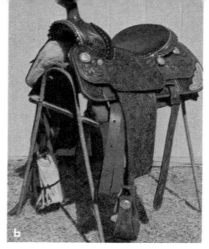

With the emphasis on pleasure riding, much has been added to the modern stock saddle to improve it over the old bucket seat types. Pictured here are: (a) Rough out work saddle. (b) Western show saddle. (c) Arab show saddle. (d) Team roping saddle.

has been placed in the skirts rather than on the tree. Many of these improvements have added to the comfort of horse and rider, but it should be also noted that many of the innovations are just window dressing. The most useful improvement in the modern stock saddle has been the free swing stirrup, which gives the rider more control of

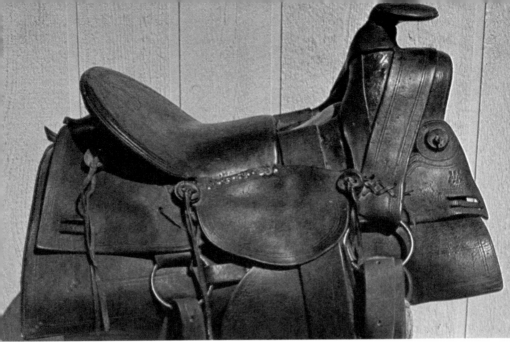

An old Texas saddle with "Sam Stagg" rigging typifies the style which added another ring just below the root of the cantle. This became the full double rig. The flat, wide Mexican horn was replaced by a more upright, round-top horn.

his legs. This stirrup is adjusted more forward on the tree than earlier saddles, and allows the rider to bend his knees and sit in the saddle, rather than be forced to practically stand in his stirrups at all times.

The forward ride saddle is also a great improvement over the old bucket seat which served its purpose to wedge the rider in one position, but allowed very little mobility. Skirt rigging allows the rider to feel more horse with his legs without feeling bulges caused by the old-style rigging dees. The in-skirt rig is safe if the skirts are well secured to the tree; many of the popular priced assembly line saddles do not have this security.

I have noticed in the past few years a trend toward a universal seat. The stock saddle rider is sitting basically in the same position as the rider in a flat saddle. Many top riders in the stock saddle classes also compete in classes over fences, which bears out the theory that there is only one way to ride a horse that is in the middle of his back regardless of the type saddle used. It is interesting to note that while the stock saddle is built in many styles, depending on its use, it is made more compact and much lighter in weight than earlier saddles. ■

CHAPTER FOUR

HOW THE STOCK SADDLE IS BUILT

The first consideration when building a saddle is the tree. There are many to choose from, depending on the type saddle to be built. Whatever type, whether for roping, cutting, barrel racing, equitation, or pleasure, the fundamental work is the same. The basic tree, unless it is one of the newer plastic trees, will be rawhide covered. This is essentially just a frame or skeleton, but it is the bone and muscle of the saddle. The old saying, "No foot, no horse," could be paraphrased as "No tree, no saddle!" The tree is all-important to the quality, integrity, and strength of the saddle, and must be constructed with care.

Placing the tree on the bench, the saddler must decide on the contour he wishes to give the seat. This is done by placing the groundwork on the tree. As the tree is just a frame, leather, or other material must be placed over the open center to give a base on which to build the seat. This is not necessary with the molded plastic tree since the ground work is built in and the tree slotted for the stirrup leathers.

The high quality tree is usually made of poplar or beech wood which is shaped, fitted, and laminated, then "ironed" or braced with metal at all points of strain. It is then covered with wet rawhide which is stitched tight all around and allowed to dry to a flint hard texture. This makes a practically indestructible tree.

The first step in placing the groundwork, is to cut a piece of heavy gauge sheet metal allowing for a space about six inches from the fork or swell at the pommel or front of the saddle, which is the area where the stirrup leather goes over the tree and which needs no filling in. The sheet metal is then cut around following a line about three inches below the top of the cantle or back of the saddle, the metal plate is then placed on the tree and bent to follow the contour of the tree. It is then removed and a piece of leather is cut to the shape of the metal plate and glued to the underside of the plate. This forms the gullet of the saddle and the leather is applied to cover the metal so that when the saddle is turned upside down, the metal plate will not show between the skirts. The leather glued to the metal plate

is cut a few inches longer to the front of the plate and folded back

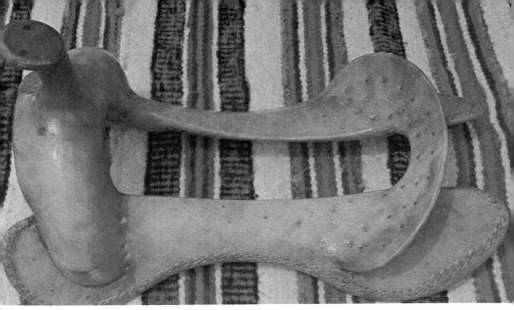

The tree is the bone and muscle of the saddle and there is a considerable variety of choice, including the new plastic types. The tree pictured here is wooden covered by "bullhide" to give maximum strength for roping.

over the top so the stirrup leathers will not rub against the bare metal. The plate is then placed on the tree, leather side down, and nailed or screwed in place around the edges and around the cantle.

The next phase depends on the quality of the saddle to be made. A top quality saddle generally will have a heavy piece of leather cut to the shape of the plate and the edges on the bottom side trimmed or skived to a feather edge. The leather then will be dampened and placed over the plate and rubbed or hammered to the contour of the metal plate. When this is dry it is given a generous coating of glue and set in place over the metal plate. In some cases it is tacked to hold it in place. Whatever padding or upholstery is added, is placed on top of this groundwork. Many saddles today are padded with foam rubber, but some high quality saddles have a piece of heavy wool felt placed on the groundwork.

The next procedure is to cover the horn. The saddle maker decides the shape he wishes to give the horn cap, which he shapes from wood or a piece of heavy leather, and places it on top of the horn fastening it with glue. Sometimes a brass wood screw is placed in the center to secure it. A piece of fairly flexible leather is then cut roughly to the shape of the horn cap and placed on the top of the horn cap allowing enough leather to wrap around the neck of the

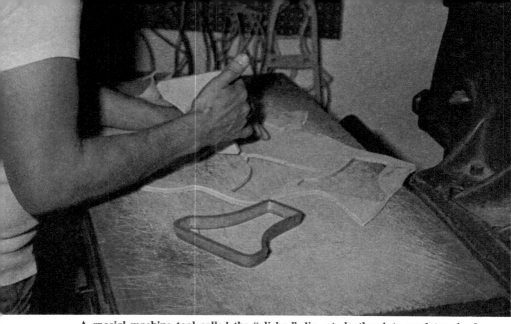

A special machine tool called the "clicker" die-cuts leather into predetermined shapes which are interchangeable on several different saddle models.

Today's quality saddles are padded with either foam rubber or heavy wool felt placed over the groundwork which has been covered by a heavy piece of leather.

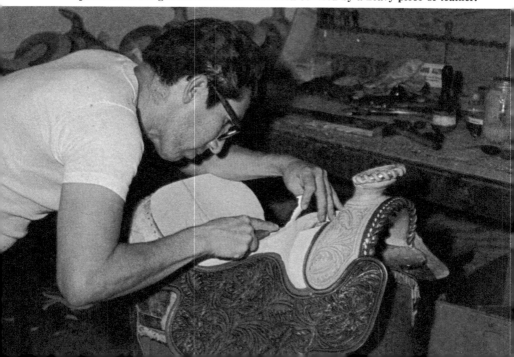

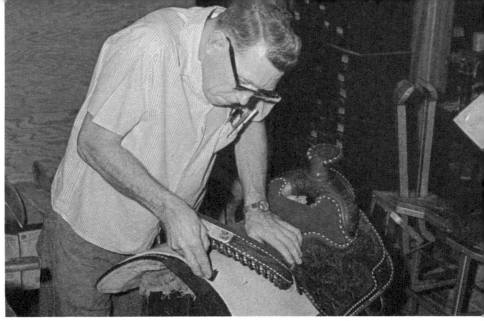

After the seat has been shaped and placed on the tree, the back of the cantle is covered with leather and the cantle binding or Cheyenne roll is stitched in place.

All that remains is to cut and tool the stirrup leathers and fenders, fit them to the tree, add the stirrups, latigos, girth or cinch and it's ready to go.

horn. A piece of leather is then cut to the shape of the underside of the horn and enough leather allowed to wrap around the neck of the horn. This excess leather is sometimes slit in strips and braided around the horn neck but in most cases it is dampened and spiral wrapped down to the fork and nailed in place. The cap cover is then stitched to the bottom piece under the horn and trimmed around the edges and polished.

The next step is to cover the fork. A piece of leather is selected that is fairly flexible and large enough to cover the fork. A hole is cut in the center for the horn, and the leather is dampened and stretched over the fork. All excess leather is pleated and these pleats are cut out; depending on the saddle maker the vee cuts are stitched together or laced. Lacing seems to be the accepted style at this time. If there is any tooling to be done on the leather, it is done at this stage. If not, the leather is nailed down around the base of the fork and a piece of leather is placed under the gullet or front of the saddle to give a finished look.

The next phase is the seat. The saddle maker selects a good piece of skirting and, wetting it, places it on the tree pressing it up to the cantle and down into the hollow of the seat; being wet, the leather is very workable and will contour and hold its new shape. The saddle maker then marks around the edges of the leather indicating the style he wishes to give the seat. He then removes the leather and, when it has dried, cuts it to shape.

When the seat is placed on the tree, the back of the cantle is covered with leather and the cantle binding or Cheyenne roll is added and stitched or laced into place. The back housing is then cut to cover the tree points at the back of the saddle. The style skirt to be used is then cut and lined with woolskin, and if the rigging is to be on the tree it will have been placed and secured with brass screws before the seat was placed. If the rigging is in the skirts, the rigging plates are set in and riveted in place before lining with woolskin.

All that remains is to cut the stirrup leather and fenders, fit them to the tree, add the stirrups and latigoes or billets, a girth or cinch, and the saddle is ready to go. The method of securing the skirts to the saddle varies, but the most usual way is to drill holes through the tree and lace the skirts through the tree. Usually the holes are drilled also through the leather that secures the rigging to the tree. If the rigging is on the tree, the lace comes through the tree and seat. It is then slit and looped through itself and a leather rosette or silver concha is added for decoration. ■

CHAPTER FIVE

THE ENGLISH OR FLAT SADDLE

The general term for any saddle other than a stock saddle is *English,* and while the term is used throughout the country, it is a misnomer. The Italians, the French, the Germans, the Poles, the Russians, and others, have made and used this *type* saddle for more than a hundred years. The term English probably originated because the English built up quite a reputation as saddle makers because they exported large quantities for saddlery and other leather goods. Also their guild or union was very strong and regulated the trade for many years. The most popular saddle today is the forward seat, or modified version of it. This saddle was actually developed by the Italians, not by the English. About sixty years ago the Italian Army started to experiment with what was considered to be a radical method of riding. There was much controversy throughout the riding world when their methods became known.

The Italian method, or seat, was a short stirrup, rider inclined forward with his upper body, stirrup leathers straight down, weight on the ball of the foot, inner calf, and thigh. This method, or seat, was ridiculed and labeled dangerous by the sit back school of riding. Over the years, however, it has become the accepted seat for any type of strenuous riding such as hunting, jumping, cross-country work, etc. The forward seat saddle has become so popular that it would be hard to find a saddle of the old type on the market today.

The English saddle makers quickly copied the style of the *Italian* saddle, as it was then known, and made many variations of the original style. The forward seat saddle differs from the earlier type flat saddles by utilizing an entirely different style tree.

The forward seat tree has the fork sloped forward, the cantle is higher, the stirrup bars are more forward on the bars of the tree, the pommel is lower and the dip of the seat or lowest part is much farther forward. This design places the rider's weight over the horse's withers where the animal is more capable of carrying weight.

A few years ago the German saddle makers put their version of the forward seat saddle on the market. It was greatly received. This type of saddle is heavier, has a much deeper seat, a heavier tree and

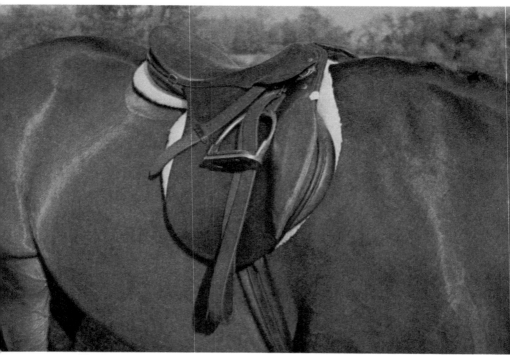

The forward seat saddle has become the accepted seat for any kind of strenuous riding such as hunting, jumping, cross-country work, etc.

is padded more fully in the panels than the Italian saddle. They finished their saddles in a deep brown color which is almost the standard today. They also added sueded or roughout leather over foam rubber to the skirt to make a comfortable and secure place behind the knee roll. A few years ago a very old and respected company of French saddlemakers came on the market with a very simple, beautifully designed saddle using a very light, thin tree, narrow seat, and lightweight leather throughout. The saddle is beautiful in its simplicity. The padding is not built up in thickness as the saddle fits close to the horse and is very flat.

This saddle was quickly adapted by professional riders and many amateurs of international ability and has become extremely popular among the show jumping people since it allows much greater mobility, which is needed over big fences. With the popularity of this saddle spreading, almost every company manufacturing saddles of the

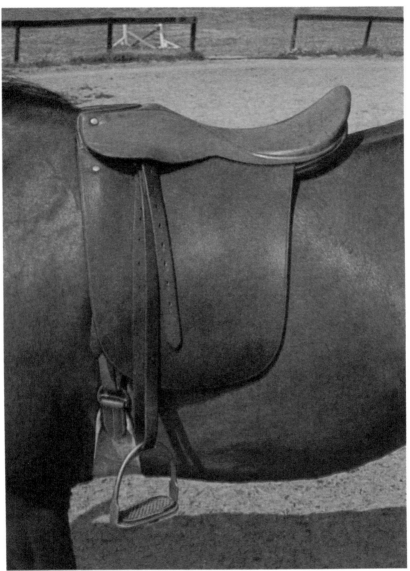

The show saddle is used primarily on our Saddlebred and Walking Horses, and has a cutback pommel to make the saddle sit low and display the horse's conformation.

jumping type, have copied it in some fashion. It is being marketed under many names and offered in practically all price ranges.

In the past few years, much saddlery has been offered from Argentina. These saddle makers have copied the Italian, German and English styles and their product has become very popular.

It seems that history is repeating itself considering that the birthplace of the saddle was the Orient. The Japanese are coming on very strong in the horse goods market.

Much saddlery has been made in India and exported to many countries of the world. This was probably due to the English influence which existed in India for so many years.

The Show Saddle

The show saddle which is used primarily today on our Saddlebred and Walking Horses, was not especially designed for this breed. It evolved from a saddle that was used extensively in England for a type horse known as a *show hack* which was generally a horse of superb conformation and way of going. This saddle was designed to show off his shoulder and entire front. The saddle was built with a cut back head and a skirt that was cut straight down from the head of the saddle to lay behind the shoulder. The seat is very flat, has a very low cantle, and vary thin padding in the panels.

The show saddle was adopted by the saddle horse people and in many cases, modified to suit their needs, but the *basic* form has not changed. ∎

CHAPTER SIX

HOW THE ENGLISH OR FLAT SADDLE IS BUILT

When building any of the many styles of flat saddle, the saddle maker must start with the tree. All flat saddle trees, regardless of style, are built primarily the same way.

Many different types of wood are utilized but they are generally built of a light weight wood such as basswood, willow or poplar. These woods are shaped by the tree maker, which is a trade or profession in itself, and the wood is laminated and glued to the shape desired. Due to the light weight and very thin construction of the flat saddle tree, it requires more ironing or bracing than the stock saddle tree. When the wood has been shaped and glued together, the entire tree is wrapped with a thin linen material which serves the same purpose as the rawhide on a stock saddle tree; it holds it together. The iron or bracing is then forged and riveted to the tree. The iron at the head, or pommel, is shaped and placed on top of the pommel and extended down the top of the fork on both sides, not quite to the tip of the fork. The iron for the underside of the fork is much heavier because this must keep the tree from spreading at the pommel. This iron is almost the width of the fork and extends to the end or tip of the fork on both sides.

The tip of the fork is fitted with a piece of heavy leather rounded and stitched double. This is what is termed as a flexible point, which prevents the points of the tree digging into the horse. The head and fork irons are then drilled together and riveted to the tree. The underside of the tree is ironed back to the root of the cantle and the cantle iron is shaped around the cantle and riveted in place. The stirrup bars are then drilled and riveted to the tree.

The saddle maker now has his tree, his next step is to install the groundwork on which to build his seat. The groundwork in a flat saddle differs from the groundwork in a stock saddle. In place of the leather and metal plate used in the stock saddle the material used in the flat saddle is linen webbing, 2½ inches wide, which is very strong but light in weight. The saddle maker chooses his webbing and begins by cutting two pieces long enough to reach from the pommel, or head of the saddle, to a point just below the middle of

When the wood tree for the English saddle has been shaped and glued together, it is wrapped with a thin linen material which reinforces it and holds it together.

the cantle. He then nails the webbing down to the tree just in front of the pommel iron. The two pieces of webbing are laid on top of each other. He spreads the webbing and nails one piece to the left of center, just below the middle of the cantle, and the other piece to the right of center.

A piece of coarse linen is cut to cover the webbing from a point about five inches from the pommel and shaped around the cantle just above the end of the webbing. This is nailed down on one side then stretched and nailed down on the opposite side. It is then nailed around the cantle.

The next procedure is to place two pads, one on each side of the tree, extending from the root of the cantle six inches along the edge of the tree bars. This builds up the edge of the tree which is directly under the edge of the seat. This wedge of padding is extremely important to the leveling of the seat, which of course means comfort for the rider. In many well built saddles of earlier vintage, this pad was made of leather, folded, tapered and hand stitched to form a leather tube. It was flared at the cantle end, and drawn more to a point toward the front of the saddle. This leather tube was stuffed with wool, dampened with water, shaped to the contour of the tree edge and nailed in place.

The next phase in building the groundwork for the English saddle is very important. A piece of webbing, the same as used to

The "groundwork" used in an English saddle consists of strips of linen webbing.

ground the seat structure, is cut around eighteen inches long and wrapped around the bar of the tree just behind the stirrup bar. About four excess inches of this webbing is allowed to hang below the edge of the tree. The webbing is then carried over the top of the seat web, pulled down, wrapped around the opposite tree bar *exactly opposite the first wrap.* This is then nailed down to the tree along the top edge with a row of heavy tacks. It is *very* important that this webbing be adjusted properly as this is the foundation to which the billet or girth straps are sewn.

The next stage concerns the placement of the seat upholstery, which today usually consists of a sheet of foam rubber. This padding is cut to the shape of the seat and secured with adhesive to the linen cover of the groundwork. A piece of wool serge is then cut roughly to the shape of the upholstered tree, stretched over it and tacked all around under the edges of the tree and over the edge of the cantle. The saddle is now ready for the leather.

A piece of good heavy pig, or hog skin is selected and cut roughly to the tree shape, allowing enough extra to fold under the tree edges all around. The leather is then thoroughly dampened with water, stretched over the tree and tacked all around. Any wrinkles are **25**

The saddler nails the webbing to the tree adding loops which become the foundation to which the billet or girth straps are sewn.

worked out until the leather is smooth and wrinkle-free, all over the seat. The leather is pleated behind the cantle to give a smooth fit, and is then allowed to dry.

While the leather is drying, the design of the jockey is decided upon and cut out. The leather which is generally used in the jockey and skirt is a nicely finished, good quality cowhide with a grain stamped on the leather to simulate pigskin. Real pigskin would be much too light in weight to use alone.

A very high quality saddle would be made by placing pigskin over the cowhide jockey and the skirt, then stitching the two together all around. This would produce a saddle covered entirely with pigskin and not many saddles of this type are offered. When they are, they will be in the top price field. When both jockeys are cut out and the seat is dry, each jockey is tacked loosely in place on the tree. A line is traced on the pigskin seat along the top of the jockeys, the jockeys are then removed and a sharp knife is used to cut along the line. When cut out, this is the basic seat, the excess leather is then removed from the tree, and the jockeys are prepared to stitch to the tree.

A piece of coarse linen is cut to cover the webbing before foam rubber padding and wool serge are added. The saddle will then be ready for the leather.

A narrow strip of very thin leather is then folded in half and whip stitched to the tops of the jockeys. This is known as the welt, which fills in the space between the seat and the jockey. When both jockeys have been furnished with the welt, the jockeys are then sewn to the seat. This is done all on the underside so that no stitching will show. When the seat is sewn to the jockeys, the seat and top edges of the jockeys are wet thoroughly with water and the seat is again stretched in place over the tree, and allowed to dry. When dry, it is removed, and side pieces are attached under each jockey with an invisible stitch which does not come all the way through the leather. These side pieces fold under the tree edge and hold the seat in place.

The seat is now wet thoroughly again and stretched over the tree. The side pieces are nailed down, the excess cut off, the wrinkles in the leather are rubbed out, and the saddle is ready for the billet or girth straps. The billet or girth straps are cut of the same quality leather as a good pair of stirrup leathers. This is a specially tanned and finished leather known in the trade as a stirrup butt. When the billets are cut out, they are stitched to the cross webbing, which was **27**

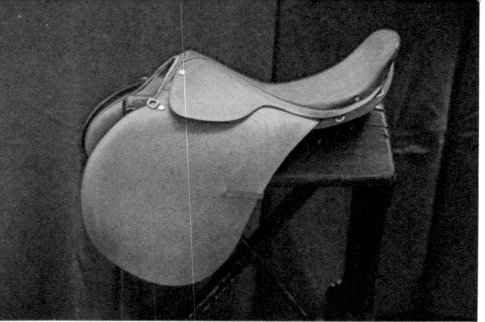

The finished product is a beautiful, custom hand-made forward seat saddle with cowhide skirts and flaps, pigskin seat and glove-hide tanned pannels.

attached across the tree, and secured behind the stirrup bars. The saddle is now ready for the skirts and panels.

As there are many styles of pannels and methods of manufacture, it would require much detail to cover all types, but without going into this detail, the foregoing explanation should provide the basics to the various methods of building flat saddles.

Race saddles and race exercise saddles are built basically the same as any type flat saddle except the trees are of much lighter construction. In the building of a race saddle, the leathers used are much thinner to keep the weight to a minimum. There is also very little padding in the pannels of an exercise saddle and not enough to mention in the lining of the race or jockey saddle.

A very popular exercise saddle is being used at the track currently. It is made of felt covered with leather, and it is very flexible and light. This saddle has only part of a tree, this consisting of an arch or fork at the pommel of the saddle to bridge the withers and stabilize the saddle from slipping from side to side. It also provides a secure place to anchor the stirrup bars. A saddle of this type is much less expensive than the full-tree saddle and will take much more punishment than the conventional exercise saddle. ■

CHAPTER SEVEN

BRIDLES AND CAVESSONS
— MARTINGALES — HALTERS

Bridles And Cavessons

The bridle or headstall, which we use to help control the horse, has in its basic form changed little in its course through the ages. Basically, it is a method of keeping the bit in place in the horse's mouth. Headstalls of leather, rope, chain and many types of webbing or cloth have been used. The same is true of reins.

Old timers in the saddlery business state that the web halter and bridle have been with us for many years. In earlier times, when horses were needed in everyday work, these web halters and bridles were called summer halters and were used only during the summer months. Also much light weight web harness was sold to be used with the family buggy or carriage. Today, much of this web is being used year round: the web halter has become very popular.

English Bridles

Today's bridles are made almost universally of leather and there are many variations. The English style bridle has changed little in the last hundred years; the only changes seem to have been in the type buckle used and in the method of securing the cheeks to the bit rings. Very early in this century the English bridle was furnished with iron buckles covered with leather. In the late twenties, bridle makers began furnishing bridles with nickel or nickel plate buckles. This, of course, was for the civilian trade, as most military saddlery was traditionally brass trimmed. About that time, the hook stud fastener became popular to secure the billet end of the cheek to the bit, this method is used universally today.

The continental style bridle has a slightly different appearance from the English, and while you would not notice it on a galloping horse, it is a different style. The adjustment differs from the English bridle at the headstall. While the English headstall has two billets and a throat latch on the crown, plus two bridle cheeks, the continental style has no adjustment on the cheeks. The cheeks are cut out of a solid strap, which has a buckle sewn in to lay at the horse's poll. **29**

The buckle is usually sewn on the half of the bridle that would be on the near side (left side) of the horse's head. The off side, or right half of the bridle, has a number of holes punched for adjustment, thus affording a way to make the bridle short or long, depending on the size of the horse's head. The billet ends, or the part which secures the bit, have buckles or hook studs. This bridle was reportedly very popular with the military. The round sewn bridles, which have become very popular recently, are made in this fashion.

In the English bridle field the variations are generally a matter of personal taste. The saddle horse group use a very narrow-width bridle and rein, plus a very wide and colorful browband. This type of bridle is sometimes furnished with a cavesson, which has the front

The hunter group uses a bridle that is made a little more stout. It has wider cheeks, wider reins and in many cases the rein is laced or braided to give a more secure grip in wet weather. Fancy bridle fronts are not favored on the hunter, either in the field or in the ring.

The other variation in the English bridle is fashioned by adding a sliphead (as it is known to the trade). This is really just another bridle cheek, which is adjusted under the headstall. The bradoon bit is attached to this second cheek when the bridle is being used as a Weymouth or full bridle. The jumper fraternity, or the group who show their horses over courses designed especially to test jumping ability, uses many modifications of the basic bridle. As decoration is not frowned upon by these people, many exhibitors use fancy colored browbands. Many styles of cavesson are also used. The dropped noseband, which is adjusted below the bit and buckled in a fashion to keep the horse's mouth closed, is very popular. The figure of eight noseband, which was primarily a racing item, is widely used. This appliance crosses above the bit, and buckles under the jaw. It is also designed to keep the mouth closed and maintain the bit in the same position in the horse's mouth at all times. Also used is the Kineton noseband. This is an affair with two metal hook-like attachments to which a noseband is buckled to span across the nose above the nostrils. The other end of the hook is attached to a sliphead arrangement, like an ordinary cavesson. The hooked attachments curve behind the bit rings, and when pressure is applied to the reins, the bit comes back against the hooks and pressure is applied to the horse's nose.

Another type cavesson, that is sometimes used on jumpers, is what is known as the anti-pulling cavesson. This consists of an ordinary cavesson, except in the specific part where the cavesson buckles behind the jaw. The anti-pulling cavesson has two pieces of curb

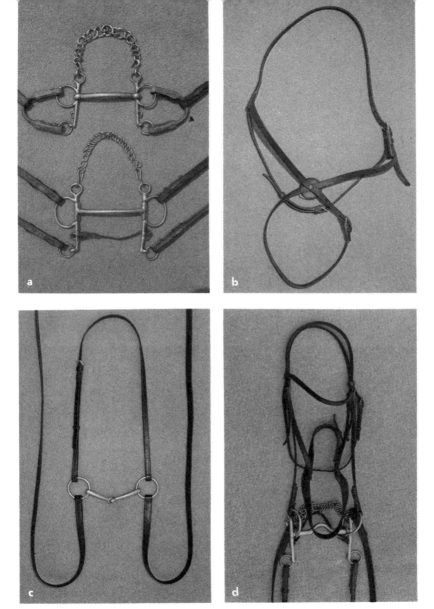

(a) The Pelham, showing the bit converter (top) for use with single rein, and the conventional use with double reins (bottom). (b) The Figure Eight noseband helps keep mouth closed. (c) Sliphead with bradoon mouthpiece sewn in. (d) The "3-in-1" Pelham with polo bit.

chain sewn one on each side in place of the buckle and billet. When in use the left side chain is attached to the right curb hook, and the right side chain is crossed over and attached to the left curb hook. As can be readily seen, this type cavesson cannot be used with a snaffle bridle.

Another item which enjoyed much popularity with the jumper and hunter set, is the shadow roll. This is, in reality, an ordinary cavesson with the front covered with sheepskin and many times stuffed (padded) to add to its size. This appliance was borrowed from the race track, where it is used extensively on the harness race horse. Sometimes, it is also used on the runner, and brush or hurdle race horse. The shadow roll is adjusted high up on the horse's nose and is supposed to prevent his seeing shadows close in front, which might cause shying. Many trainers of hunters have used this appliance at one time or another to make a timid or cheating horse stand back and jump his fences, rather than get in close, prop and then jump. Many trainers attribute the success of their horses to this device, however this has always been a point of debate.

Many jumper riders use another item borrowed from the running tracks — rubber rein grips. These consist of tubes of pimpled rubber which are backed with cloth. The reins are pulled through these tubes which are then stitched to the reins. This allows the rider a very secure grip.

The round-sewn bridle has enjoyed great popularity lately in all phases of flat saddle riding. The German saddlery manufacturers "reincarnated" this bridle which is sewn round except for the adjusting billets and the billets which secure the bit. Matching round-sewn martingales and breastplates are also very popular. Due to the labor involved in handsewing, this style bridle and accessory is quite expensive.

The gag bridle is also much used by the jumper people, and lately the gag has been adopted by the cutting horse and reining fraternity. The gag bridle was borrowed from the polo enthusiast and is a bridle which has many variations. Basically, it is a pulley affair which, upon pulling on the reins, draws the bit up in the horse's mouth, while pressure is applied at the poll or top of the head where the headstall lays. Some types of gag bridles were designed to be used in conjunction with other bits such as snaffles or curbs. Other types were used alone as single bits, many times an extra pair of reins were attached to the snaffle type gag, and the horse was ridden on this rein unless stronger control was needed, then the gag rein was applied. This bridling arrangement was used

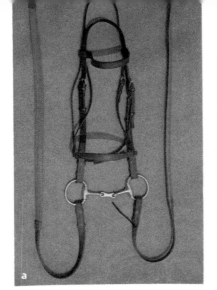

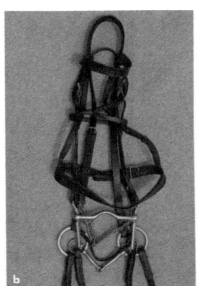

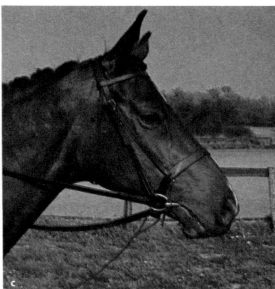

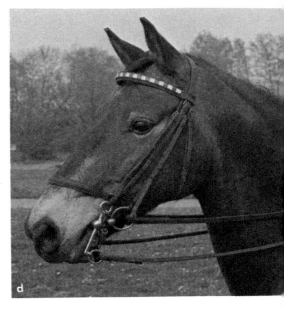

(a) Hunting bridle with Dr. Bristol snaffle with egg-butt rings and rubber rein grips. (b) The Weymouth or full bridle showing both curb and bradoon mouthpieces. (c) The full-cheek snaffle. (d) The Weymouth shown in use.

where quick sharp control was needed and it is much used as a training device.

Draw reins are another tack item borrowed from the polo player, they are actually reins of any width that are double the length of an ordinary rein. The rein has a buckle to connect the two reins just as a conventional snaffle rein. The opposite end of the rein is fashioned in a loop which is wide enough to allow a girth to pass through. The girth is passed through each loop end and adjusted one on each side of the horse. The opposite end of the rein is then passed through the ring of the bit, and thence back to the rider's hand. This appliance is generally used with a snaffle bit, and the horse is ridden on a regular snaffle rein. The draw rein is used for stronger control, somewhat as a curb rein would be used in a double rein bridle.

Due to the powerful leverage which the draw reins and gags exert on the horse's mouth, they require careful handling. They are effective only when used properly.

The race bridle, or running horse type, as used in the United States, differs from the types used in England and on the European Continent. The American style bridle is fashioned out of doubled or lined and stitched leather, and consists of a slip type headstall plus a separate throat latch. The reins most used are made with a loop or keeper stitched at the bit end. The rein is looped around the bit and through the keeper to secure the rein to the bit. The reins are always furnished with rubber hand parts. Many bridles are also furnished with hook studs or buckle billets. The fashion in England and Continental Europe is a conventional type English bridle. The rubber rein grips are used, however.

Western Or Stock Horse Bridle

The western bridle, to use a broad term, covers all of the styles used today on stock-type horses. There are so many styles available that there are almost too many to catalog. Every manufacturer of stock horse equipment manufactures a different style; every year someone introduces something new. These bridles can be constructed of braided leather, or doubled and stitched leather. They can be silver mounted, or buckstitched, or thonged with contrasting colors of leather. They can be one-ear style, or two-ear style, either of them with or without throat latch. They can be sewn round with silver trim, have chain reins, mohair reins, plain rope — you name it, they have it.

Basically there are only two original patterns which go back to early style stock horse bridles. The Texas-style was originally

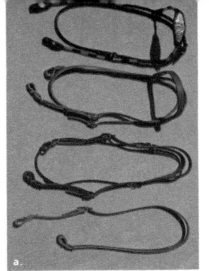
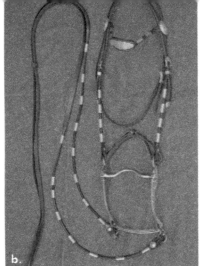

(a) Various Western headstalls showing (top to bottom) a silver bridle with browband, one-ear headstall with throat latch, leather headstall with browband, and a split-ear headstall. (b) A silver-mounted Western show bridle. (c) A silver show bridle showing silver bit and silver-mounted reins.

furnished with a browband, throat latch and some type of noseband. The Texas-style reins were always split, that is, not secured at the center with a buckle or other means. The basic reason behind split reins is connected with the horse being taught to ground tie, as the Texas-style riding advocates. Thus the reins only need be released, and the horse is "anchored at that very spot."

The California-style bridle is vastly different from bridle types used in other parts of the country. While the Texas-style bridle migrated west, north and east, the California-style moved up the Pacific coast but did not become very popular east of the Rockies. The California-style bridle has changed (basically) very little from the early Spanish and Mexican influence. Most styles are of braided rawhide, using rawhide buttons as fasteners. Many of these bridles are one of a kind. Many very colorful bridles in the California-style are made of braided horse hair. The California bridle is always furnished with reins that are joined in the center, and fitted with a quirt-like appliance known as a *romal*. The joined reins are not designed to ground tie, as the California-style rider carries a pair of hobbles with which to anchor his horse.

Martingales

A number of other appliances are used with bridles to help train or restrain the horse. Among these are martingales, also known as tie downs. The standing martingale consists of a strap with a loop sewn at one end, plus a looped-in buckle at the opposite end. The loop-end is adjusted to the cavesson, and the buckle-end slips over the girth, adjustment is at the buckle end. A neck yoke or strap is also furnished with a buckle adjustment and a loop at the bottom of the yoke for the martingale to slip through. The standing martingale can be adjusted to limit the elevation of the horse's head.

Another variation of the standing martingale is the polo-pattern. This type is generally made a little more stout than the regular martingale and has the buckle adjustment at the chest level of the horse, rather than at the girth.

The running martingale has a fork at the end opposite the girth loop and has two rings sewn one at the end of each fork. The reins slide through the rings, and the riders can, to some extent, control the elevation of the horse's head. This appliance allows more freedom than the standing martingale. The running martingale is also furnished with a neck strap or yoke.

The Irish martingale consists of a short strap with a ring sewn in each end. It is used by sliding over the reins under the horse's

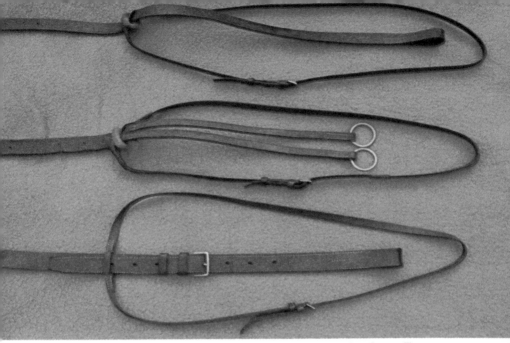

Martingales, also known as tie-downs, are used to train or restrain a horse. From top to bottom: the ordinary standing martingale, the running or ring martingale, and the polo-pattern variety.

throat, and it prevents both reins from ending up on the same side of the horse's neck, but does not limit the elevation of the head.

Using the running martingale or the Irish type, a leather or heavy rubber martingale stop is sometimes used. This is placed on the rein and adjusted between the martingale ring and the bit to prevent the ring of the martingale catching in the buckle or stud fastening the rein-end to the bit.

Recently a martingale of sorts has become rather popular with the jumper people. It is a variation of the gag and draw reins, and its action somewhat combines the effect of both. It consists of a strap that loops over the girth in the same fashion as an ordinary martin-gale. The ends are forked or split and passed through the bit rings one on each side. They are then carried back and buckle one to each rein. Special reins are furnished with buckles sewn on at spaced intervals for adjustment.

Side reins, which are used to help set the head of a young horse, or to help "make a mouth," as it is termed, are leather straps which buckle or snap to the bit rings and loop over the girth one on each

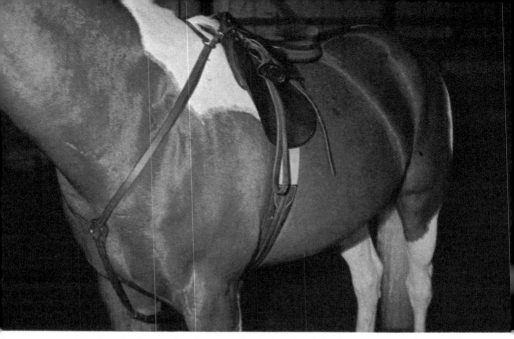

The hunting breastplate is primarily designed to help keep the saddle from sliding back. Martingale lead-up straps are sometimes buckled to the chest ring.

side of the horse. These appliances quite often have a heavy elastic insert in the bit end of the rein which allows some flexibility to the head and neck. It is much more effective to use than a fixed leather rein.

The hunting breastplate is another appliance that fits somewhat in the martingale category. This consists of a neck yoke arrangement that has a strap which leads up from the girth and terminates in a ring or dee ring at the chest. From this ring, there are two straps which lead up to the withers; these straps each terminate in a small ring. A strap is stitched to each of these rings and lays across the withers, this completes the yoke. Two adjustable straps lead from the rings at the withers, and are buckled to the dees on each side of the saddle pommel. This breastplate is primarily designed to help keep the saddle from sliding back. Martingale lead-up straps are sometimes adjusted or buckled to the chest ring. There are two types: a standing type lead-up strap, or a running-type martingale. This breast plate is quite often made up in sewn round style or double and stitched.

The breast collar, or polo pattern breast girth, as it is sometimes known, is also designed to help keep the saddle in place. It consists of a folded and padded leather breast piece with a lay of leather sewn down the center on the top side, terminating at a dee ring at each end. An adjustable strap is attached to each dee ring to loop around the girth. Another adjustable strap is generally attached to the breast piece which passes over the withers of the horse to hold the breast collar in place.

The western stock horse uses this same appliance, but with many variations. The western style is very often curved and shaped, tooled, carved, or buckstitched. Also, many breast collars are made of braided mohair or nylon in brilliant colors with matching cinches or girths. However they are made or decorated, they all serve the same purpose.

Halters

Halters, or head collars as the English term them, are various styles of strap work (web, rope or other material) fashioned to fit the head of the horse in order to control or restrain him when he is not wearing a bridle. The rope or sash-cord type halter has given way to a superior nylon or plastic rope-like material. They are furnished in many colors and have become extremely popular. The design, however, is primarily the same. They are fashioned from a single length of rope material threaded through special hardware which results in a very strong halter. The nose piece is the only separate piece in the design. The leather halter is probably the most popular.

The basic leather halter is made up in many styles. Some are buckstitched, others are silver mounted. Yet others are embossed to simulate reptile or other exotic leathers. Overall, the most popular style is what is termed the Newmarket pattern, which is usually double and stitched, or three row stitched with round throat latch, and a double buckle crown. This type halter is almost universally used. Many halters are made up with snaps on the throat latch to eliminate unbuckling the crown piece in order to remove it from the horse.

The nylon web halter has become very popular recently. This halter is made up very much as the leather halter, except nylon web is used in place of leather straps. These halters are furnished in all shades of the rainbow, and are very strong. They apparently give good service for a moderate price.

Also in the halter category is the longeing or breaking cavesson and the chambon. Both these appliances are used when longeing, or as it is known at the track, "the gyp line." The horse can be longed

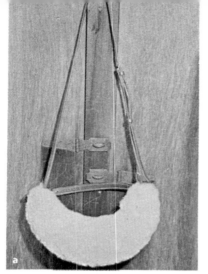
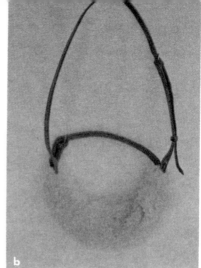
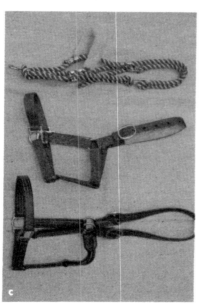

(a) A dropped noseband is used to keep mouth closed. The protective sheepskin is not in use much anymore. (b) The shadow-roll rides higher on the nose and is used a great deal in harness racing and with some jumpers. (c) Various halters showing (top to bottom) a nylon rope variety with protective sheepskin guard for nose, a nylon web halter, and the popular leather type. (d) The longeing cavesson is preferred by most professionals.

The chambon combines the principles of the gag, the snaffle, and the martingale. It exerts tension on the mouth when head is raised past certain point.

off the halter or in a bridle, but most professionals prefer a longeing cavesson. This consists of a headstall made up slightly heavier than a riding bridle. The cheeks differ from the ordinary bridle cheek. While they buckle to the headstall billet in the conventional manner they are split at the bottom of the cheek and buckle to a hinged set of metal plates that will conform to the horse's nose. These metal plates are furnished with three rings, one at the front in the center of the nose piece plus another ring on each side. This allows the longe line to be buckled in three positions. Or, a pair of side lines can be attached to the side rings and then lead back to a surcingle. The longe is attached at the front of the plate. The noseband to which the metal noseplates are attached is heavily padded and covered with soft leather to protect the horse's nose from injury.

The chambon in its true form is used very little in the United

States, but is used extensively all over Europe. The chambon consists basically of a conventional bridle fitted with a snaffle bit. At the top of the headstall, just below the browband, a gag runner or ring is attached, one on each side of the headstall. The body of the chambon consists of a cord or flat leather strap (similar to a martingale leadup) which attaches to the girth or surcingle, passes between the horse's forelegs and terminates in a ring or dee ring. Two cords, or strap Y pieces, are adjusted to this (chest) ring and a cord or strap is carried up and through the gag runner, on each side of the horse's head. This strap is then carried down and snapped or buckled to the rings of the snaffle bit. There is usually an adjustment to shorten or lengthen the branched parts of the chambon. This appliance is used to bring down the horse's head and make him mechanically use his hind legs farther under his center of gravity. This device exerts tension on the mouth when the horse raises his head above the level to which the trainer has adjusted the chambon. The chambon is almost never used in mounted training, as a fractious horse could possibly bring himself down if he were to fight the device. A variation of this appliance is used by some cutting horse trainers to bring the head down. The variation used is a browband made of chain to which the cords or leather are attached. The theory being that when the horse raises his head, the chain draws tight and he lowers his head to relieve the tension. This device is sometimes called a brain chain.

While the classic school of horsemanship frowns on many of these appliances, much has probably been accomplished by their use, but only in the hands of a skilled and careful horseman. ■

CHAPTER EIGHT

HORSE BOOTS — GIRTHS — STIRRUPS — SPURS

Boots

Horse boots, as they are termed, are made up of many materials and for many uses. The Standardbred trotter or pacer probably has more variety of boots than any other horse. Depending on his gait, and the problem he may encounter going at racing speed, he may wear any or all of the following appliances: knee boots with elastic suspenders to keep them in place, front shin and tendon boots, quarter boots and elbow boots. On the hind legs he may wear hind shin boots with hock, ankle and speedy cut protection. Any and all of these boots can be made up of leather, plastic, felt, rubber or any combination of these materials. The running horse usually does not wear such a variety of boots. Elastic bandages most often take the place of a boot. Some horses may wear a tendon boot or a rundown boot, if he has a tendency to grab or catch himself with the toes of his hind feet. The Saddlebred horse and the Tennessee Walker may wear a quarter boot which in most cases is lead weighted. This boot is more often used to increase the action of the horse rather than for protection. Many jumpers wear a rubber bell boot which protects the heel and coronet area. The light tendon and galloping boot is also used on occasion.

The stock horse (if he wears a boot) wears skid boots on the hind ankles which protect the fetlocks from abrasion when executing a sliding stop.

Girths

The saddle girth is made in many styles, and of many materials. The most popular western girth, or cincha, is generally made of braided cord or rope. Better quality and higher priced girths are fashioned out of woven or braided mohair and/or nylon. Leather has not been used very much in the manufacture of the western girth. Recently, however, a patented girth has been placed on the market which is made of folded, padded leather with heavy elastic inserts. A leather safe is placed over the elastic and buckles. This looks like it could be quite an improvement over the existing western girth. **43**

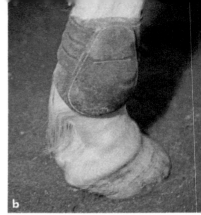
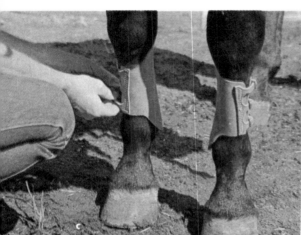
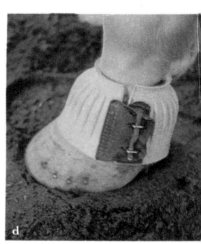

Horse boots are made up of many materials and for many uses: (a) Skid boots for the stock horse to protect hind ankles. (b) Ankle boots protect against interfering (c) Splint boots. (d) Rubber bell boots protect coronet and heel.

The English or flat saddle type girth is more varied. The standard is a folded girth of baghide leather which is furnished with or without elastic. Sometimes there is a preference to have the elastic placed at both ends of the girth. This gives the horse more breathing room and maintains the same girth tension at all times. Many girths are made in a shaped pattern. This consists of a leather girth which is cut narrow behind the horse's elbows, it is padded and has a leather strap stitched down the center for reinforcement. This girth is very popular at the running tracks. When used as an exercise girth, it is always furnished with an elastic insert.

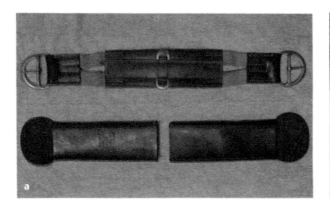

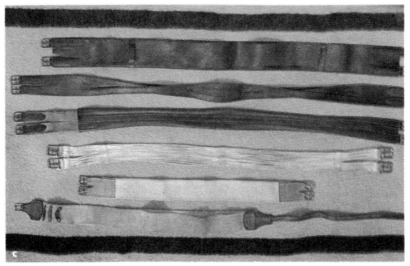

Saddle girths are made in many styles, and of many materials: (a) The elastic girth with slip-over leather protectors. (b) The braided mohair and nylon Western girth. (c) From top down: the Fitzwilliams girth, Balding girth, Shaped girth with elastic, Nylon string girth, Elastic web girth, Race girth and overgirth.

The Balding girth is a solid strap leather girth which is slit to divide the girth in three equal parts. The three straps are then crossed over in the center of the girth. A leather shield is placed over the crossover, and is padded and stitched at the girth center. This girth was primarily a polo invention, to minimize girth pinch- **45** ing behind the elbow.

The web type, English style girths are most often made of a material which is known as union web. This is a web woven of linen and wool. Many girths are also made of heavy linen which is woven in tubular form, then pressed flat before attaching the buckles. This provides a very strong girth.

The humane girth is made up of webbing, or leather, and differs from other types of girth by a fitting sewn at each end that allows the girth buckles to be sewn to a sliding strap which adjusts to the movement of the horse.

Many of the web girths are lined with rubber which is pimpled, much in the same manner as the rubber rein grips used in racing. This retards the girth from slipping. Girths made up in this fashion are primarily aimed at the saddle horse trade. The cut back show saddle quite often utilizes this same type rubber lining on the saddle pannels to prevent slipping.

The Fitzwilliams girth is a very safe style, it is made up in leather or web as a conventional girth, but has an extra girth of strap leather which is run through loops on top of the girth. This combination has six girth buckles which allows the use of all of the saddle billets.

The jockey uses a different type girthing arrangement, the material universally used is elastic web. As the race saddle generally has only one billet strap, the short girth is made up of two layers of elastic web and furnished with a buckle at each end. Also a surcingle, or overgirth, is used which is made of the same material except that it is furnished with a buckle and billet. It is 'made long enough to go all the way around the horse and over the top of the saddle. The jumper rider, participating in international competition, also uses the elastic overgirth.

Stirrups

These devices are quite difficult to catalog inasmuch as there are so many variations. The metal (flat saddle) type, although they look a great deal the same, are furnished in many styles. The shape of the sides, the pattern of the tread, the weight, and the metal used varies in the many diverse styles. It would require many pages to run down all of the varieties used throughout the world, as each country has contributed many styles and patterns.

This same problem exists when trying to catalog the western stirrup. Aside from the fact that they are made of leather covered wood, it is almost impossible to run down all patterns and styles which range from the simple ox bow pattern to the heavy, broad, dog

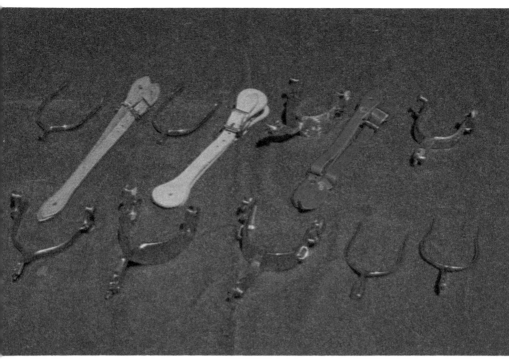

Spurs range from the heavy, ornate, roweled types to the very simple spur that is becoming more and more popular today.

house type. These stirrups are made in many styles and their popularity is generally a matter of locality and function.

Spurs

The basic spur originated as a thorn attached to the heel of the rider. From this simple device, all manner of spurs evolved, and these range from the heavy, ornate, richly decorated, roweled type to the very plain, simple spur that is becoming popular today. Spurs at one time denoted the social level of the wearer: Knights wore gold, Pages wore silver, and the lower order of horsemen donned simple iron spurs. ■

CHAPTER NINE

THE HISTORY OF THE BIT

There seems to be a great variation of basic types and styles of bits. Yet, when scrutinized more closely, it is apparent that there are only two basic types, the *curb* and the *snaffle*. The latter is sometimes called the *bradoon* (British). All variations, styles and patterns evolve from these two basic bits (mouthpieces).

The bit is not a modern invention, as some might think. It is evident that a snaffle bit, very much like the ones in use today, had been developed by horsemen centuries before Christ. The workmanship was rather crude by comparison, but the design was almost identical with today's O-ring snaffle widely used by English riders.

Drawings and photographs of actual display items taken from an exhibition of equestrian equipment at the Metropolitan Museum of Art show an astounding variation of bitting apparatus ranging back as far as 500 B.C. While some appear to be simply and forthrightly designed, others are ornate in the extreme, including heraldic coats of arms, exotic birds, enameled knobs, crescentic openings, gilded tabs, serpents, horned masks, and just about every other decoration imaginable. The interesting point is that all of the earlier bits were of the snaffle variety. The curb bit made its debut during the reign of the Tudors and quickly spread to all parts of Europe.

A study of methods employed by the North-American Indians gives us an insight which is perhaps the most revealing of all regarding the truly ancient forms of equine bitting. They wrapped a length of rawhide around the lower jaw of their horses, passing it through the mouth, under the tongue and tied it below the jaw at a point where the reins were also affixed. The fact that it was effective is supported by the truth that the North-American Indians came to be recognized as some of the most superb light cavalry "troops" the world had ever known.

The rawhide bosal and the spade bit were contributed to the Americas by the Spaniards early in the 16th and 17th Centuries, A.D. The Spaniards were stockmen, and their horses had to be adept at handling cattle — for starting, stopping and dodging. Thus the basic

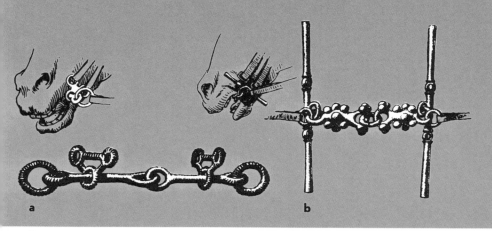

Drawings and photographs of display items shown at the Metropolitan Museum of Art show snaffle type bits ranging back to the fifth century B.C. (a) A Roman snaffle bit 500-300 B.C. (b) Roman snaffle bit IV Century A.D.

The curb bit made its debut during the reign of the Tudors in England and quickly spread to other parts of Europe. Note spade-like characteristics shown in photo of XV Century curb bit.

principles of Western horsemanship were formed along with the tack which was required to make it most effective.

The Spanish and Mexican traditions were carried on by the Californians, who in turn added their modifications. These same traditions were carried into Texas, and for years the Texans used the "Jaquima" as a training tool. In the meantime, the snaffle and curb bits had been brought to our shores by the English and other Northern Europeans. This Eastern influence travelled west and south, invading Texas and gradually replaced the bosal and spade bit there. Wherever the snaffle bit was used in early training, it was almost always followed by the curb bit. When early training was done with the bosal (Jaquima) it was most usually followed by the spade bit. These traditions carry into today's horseworld with the Spanish and Mexican school of thought predominant on the West Coast, while the snaffle/curb approach is prevalent in most sections of the country east of the Rocky Mountains. ■

CHAPTER TEN

PRINCIPLES OF CONTROL

There is a great deal of information offered on the subject of bits, and it is unfortunate that much of it is in error. Bits constitute a most important part of equine control, and there are altogether too many "horsemen" who rely upon what a particular bit did for another horse rather than individually studying the needs of each horse. It is also an error to rigidly stick with "Western" type bits just because the horse is a stock type animal and ridden under a western saddle. This also holds true the other way around for the English horse. We should worry more about results than appearances. In order to understand what different bits do, one must first analyze the anatomy of the horse's head and mouth, then relate it to some of the basic laws of physics.

When one compares the physical stature and muscular capacity of man to that displayed by the horse, it is certainly evident that man cannot barehandedly overpower and thus control his horse. Man exercises control by applying his intellect to a training program which convinces the horse that man *can* overpower him when and if he should choose to do so. To this end, man must pinpoint an applied force onto a particularly sensitive part of the horse's anatomy. The most convenient part of the horse's anatomy which offers a variety of sensitive areas is the horse's head. It is also true that if one controls a horse's head he controls the horse. Man must, therefore, design a device which enables him to apply various degrees of pressure to these sensitive areas when he deems it prudent to do so. The device, of course, is the bridle which consists of a headstall and reins, plus either a bit which goes into the mouth, or a nosepiece as used with the hackamore. A great variety of these "devices" have been designed and built, and all of them utilize one or more of the seven basic points of control located on the horse's head. The *tongue* is the first of these points. No matter the type of mouthpiece used, the tongue will usually receive a certain amount of pressure.

The second point of control consists of the *bars*. These essentially are those portions of the jaw bones which lie inside the mouth and between the front (incisor) and the back (molar) teeth. These areas are devoid of teeth, and are thinly covered with very sensitive flesh. So sensitive, in fact, that a great deal of care must be exercised not to deaden their feeling, thus impeding the responsiveness exhibited by the horse when pressures are applied to these areas.

The *lips* constitute the third point of control. They are thinly covered with skin and are very sensitive to any pressure. It is this area of control which is most affected when the snaffle bit is used. In order to prevent injury to the lips at the corners of the mouth, either rubber or leather bit guards should be used. This eliminates an excessive pinching or cutting action displayed by some bit types.

Another area where the skin is quite sensitive is known as the *curb groove*. It is located between the jaw bones on the underside of the horse's head, and it is this area which is affected by the action of the curb strap.

The fifth point of control is at the top of the horse's head in an area called the *poll*. It is the only point of control that comes into play with the halter. The crownpiece of most headstalls passes directly over the poll, and its action is best visualized by considering the action of the gag bit, which is rigged so that the crownpiece exerts pressure on the poll as the jointed, snaffle mouthpiece is drawn into the corners of the lips.

Number six on the list of control points is the horse's *nose*. This is the point that comes into play with the use of the hackamore, and with certain types of curb bit headstalls. These devices utilize a nosepiece which wraps over the horse's nose. The structure of bone and skin on the equine nose is extremely sensitive. So sensitive, in fact, that one can obtain different responses merely by varying the texture of the material from which these nosepieces are made. Sheepskin coverings are undoubtedly the mildest, while braided leather would exhibit a greater degree of control. The narrower the nosepiece, the more control because a force imparted to this device by rein pressure would be spread over a lesser area than would be the case if a wide one were to be used. Again care must be used, for horses' noses have been broken by the indiscriminate use of excessive force.

The seventh point of control is on each side of the *lower jaw* back of the curb groove. Once again it can be noted that the skin is quite thinly structured over the bone, and this is an indicator of sensitiveness as can be demonstrated by tapping yourself on the shinbone, and comparing your nerve responses to those induced by tapping on the fleshy part of the leg. The lower jaw is the primary

A great variety of control devices have been designed and built, and all of them utilize one or more of the seven basic points of control located on the head.

point of control when the rawhide bosal is in use. If one uses too much force with the bosal, it can remove skin from the jaw!

Now that the seven points of control have been located and defined, it is up to each horseman to select the device which will best suit the horse he is riding. It should be remembered that many horses will exhibit a changing need. For example, one might be required to go back to a jointed, snaffle mouthpiece used in conjunction with draw reins, if a horse sours on the curb bit arrangement. Injuries to one or more points of control might also occasion the temporary switch to another type mouthpiece, nosepiece or headstall. ■

CHAPTER ELEVEN

THE SNAFFLE (BRADOON) BIT

While there are those who would include the hackamore when defining the various kinds of bits, the purist would claim that it is a somewhat different kind of device. The word *bit* is best defined as the mouthpiece part of the bridle, together with the adjacent parts to which the reins attach. The mechanical hackamore would fit this description if one wanted to widen the meaning to include the word *nosepiece* along with or in place of the word *mouthpiece*. Thus one might state that horsemen use three kinds of "bits." In order to avoid confusion, each of these types are treated separately; first the snaffle, or bradoon, followed by the curb and the hackamore in their respective chapters.

Most snaffles are mild bits, having jointed mouthpieces with O-rings or D-rings at the ends. They exert control through action on the tongue, and on the corners of the mouth. The action on the tongue is a "nutcracker" effect caused by hinging in its middle as force is applied to the reins. The effect on the corners of the mouth is caused by the direct pressure of the metal mouthpiece on the sensitive skin tissue as the pull on the reins is increased. The snaffle does not exert any pressure on the nose, curb groove, jaws or bars. Nor does it exert any influence through pressure on the poll, unless it is rigged as a gag bit, or if the headstall is improperly adjusted.

The severity of snaffles can be increased by making them out of twisted wire or several links of chain. The severity of the regular, jointed snaffle can be varied by increasing or decreasing the diameter of the bit at its ends. The smaller it is, the more severe its action will be.

When selecting a snaffle bit, it is important to remember just how it works on the tongue and on the corners of the mouth. Snaffle bits are curved, and the greater this curve or the tighter the joints where it hinges, the less intense the nutcracker action will be on the tongue. If you want the maximum nutcracker action, choose a straight arm mouthpiece with a very loose joint.

The snaffle is frequently referred to as a *colt bit* because it is very often chosen as the first bit for a young horse in training. The snaffle

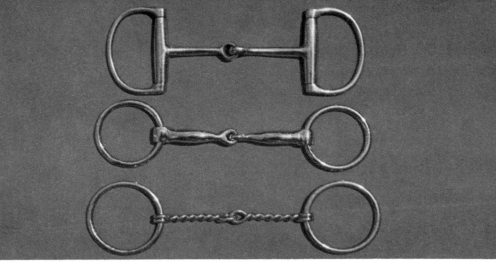

Most snaffles are mild bits, having jointed mouthpieces with O-rings or D-rings at their ends. Control is achieved by action on tongue and corners of mouth.

bit does not touch the bars of the mouth, an area so important in later training, thus one does not run the risk of damaging them if the young horse should decide to fight his bit. The action of the snaffle can be lessened for training purposes by inserting the mouthpiece through a soft rubber tube, or by wrapping it in a soft, pliable piece of leather. This increases the diameter of the *canons* of the bit so that the bearing surface is increased where it touches the corners of the mouth. This soft material also lessens the nutcracker effect and cushions any abrasive pressure occasioned by head tossing or by heavy hands.

The snaffle bit mouthpiece is sometimes combined with other forms, as in the Pelham bit where a combination snaffle and curb arrangement is used. It is equipped for use with two sets of reins. One set attaches to a set of rings found at the ends of the mouthpiece. The other set of reins attaches to a set of rings located further down at the ends of the cheekpieces. The upper set of reins would be used like regular snaffle reins, while the lower set would be for more severe action when the occasion demanded a firmer control. The "Weymouth" is another combination form. It is also referred to as the *full* or *double* bridle, and employs two separate bits, one being the snafflle and the other the curb.

All in all, the snaffle is a very effective bit. If it is designed and used correctly, it makes an excellent training device and can be brought into action whenever re-schooling is called for. ■

CHAPTER TWELVE

THE CURB BIT

The *curb bit* is the most popular type used on Western horses. It is also employed as part of the design approach to the Pelham and Weymouth bits so popular with English riders. It was previously suggested that the basic laws of physics be related to the design of equine control devices. While the gag bit type of rigging displays a "pulley-like" arrangement, the curb bit uses the mouth as a fulcrum point, applying pressure on both the poll and the curb groove. The leverage advantage given to the rider by most curb bits falls in the range of two to one, thus a two inch movement of the reins will cause both the curb strap and the headstall to be shortened by one inch. This shortening exerts a pressure on three control points: the mouth, the curb groove, and the poll. Then, depending on the design of the mouth-piece, that portion of the pressure applied to the mouth might, in turn, be divided between the bars and the tongue. It is therefore apparent that the control exerted by a curb bit bridle can be designed to apply force to as many as four of the seven total points of control. This does not take into consideration the fact that special nose band arrangements are available which would add a fifth point of control — the very sensitive nose. Above all, it should be remembered that if the rider should apply a force of fifty pounds to the reins, and through leverage have this multiplied at least twice, the horse would feel a total pressure of one hundred or more pounds.

Did you ever lie prone and try to rise while someone concentrated a five pound pressure on a string run across the bridge of your nose? Try it! It's a revealing example of what a small amount of force can do to a sensitive area. It will also convince almost anyone that moderation should be used when pulling at the reins. Heavy hands and anger can cause intense pain and bewilderment to your horse. Remember this, it is *important!*

The cheeks of the curb bit employ the use of long shanks. The upper ends attach to the headstall, and the lower ends provide means for attachment to the reins. The curb strap is most often attached to the same rings which anchor the headstall, although some cheek-

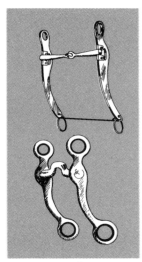

The leverage advantage given to the rider by most curb bits is in the range of two to one. Control pressure is applied to the mouth, the curb groove and the poll.

pieces provide separate loops for this purpose. The amount of pressure applied to the various points of control depends upon the ratio of measurements taken from the mouthpiece to either end of the cheekpiece, multiplied by the force applied to the reins. When one considers the strength in the arms of almost any rider, multiplied by the leverage advantage given by the curb bit arrangement, and remembers that this multiplied force is applied to concentrated points of control on exquisitely sensitive equine tissue, is there any wonder that the horse silently screams "uncle" and does what his rider wants? Again one pleads for the light, sensitive, give and take hands of the understanding, compassionate horseman.

Curb bit cheekpieces offer another option — the fixed mouthpiece or loose jaw design. Fixed mouthpiece curb bits have the mouthpiece and the cheekpieces welded, bolted or riveted so that they are rigidly positioned in relationship to one another; if one part of the fixed mouthpiece bit moves, it all moves. The loose jaw bit allows a certain amount of movement of either of the cheekpieces without affecting the mouthpiece, or the other cheekpiece. This type was originated by the old Spanish bitmasters, and was considered to be a superior design because it was more flexible, which lessened the severity of lateral tugs imposed by rein movement. There is also evidence that 57 loose jaw types occasion the horse to create more mouth moisture than do the fixed mouthpiece types. Adequate mouth moisture protects tissue and preserves the sensitiveness so important to bit response.

Curb Bit Mouthpieces

The curb bit is comprised of three elements — the mouthpiece, the cheekpieces and the curb strap. Of these three, the mouthpiece is probably the subject of most controversy. The primary pressure bearing surfaces of the horse's mouth are provided by the bars and by the tongue. The mildest bit would be one which conforms to the contour of these surfaces. This would be the low or medium port mouthpiece, although the straight or plain port mouthpiece is considered to be the mildest by most horsemen. If one wants to increase the pressure on the tongue, use the straight mouthpiece. If you want to relieve the pressure on the tongue, while increasing it on the bars, go to the higher port types.

There is yet another way to alter the severity of the mouthpiece. The greater the diameter of the mouthpiece, the less severe it will be. This is because the bearing surface is increased and any given force will be distributed over a wider area of sensitive tissue. It would be akin to changing that string across the bridge of your nose to a half inch rope (see second paragraph, this chapter). The discomfort would be greatly lessened!

There are those who believe that the high port mouthpiece actually comes in contact with the roof of the horse's mouth. This is not true. The port would have to be three and one half or four inches long before it could contact the roof of the mouth. The action of these mouthpieces is divided between the tongue and the bars, no other part of the mouth. The higher the port, the more tongue relief and the greater the pressure on the bars.

Some people, who have never used a cricket mouthpiece, believe that the cricket increases the severity of the bit. This is not a valid assumption if the mouthpiece is properly designed. It's primary purpose is to act as a "pacifier." The cricket should be large enough to almost completely fill the space provided by the curve of the port. A cricket that is too small, or placed too high in the port will pinch the tongue and defeat the purpose of its design. It is also desirable that the cricket be copper plated. Copper increases the flow of saliva which keeps a mouth moist and sensitive.

The spade mouthpiece presents a subject complex enough to fill an entire book by itself. It is extremely popular on the West Coast, where many great horses have been trained. The true spade bit will often have an extremely high port, sometimes as much as four and one half inches. A roller or cricket is employed to give a chirping sound which the horse finds to be both pleasant and soothing, and substantial amounts of copper assure a flow of saliva necessary to the sensitive mouth. Copper wires are often worked into the design so that they extend from the side of the spade to the point where the mouthpiece attaches to the cheeks. The cheekpieces come in myriad sizes, shapes and lengths, depending on the specific results the trainer is striving to achieve.

The extremely long port is balanced so that it "forces" the horse to flex at the poll, thus achieving the proper head position. The angle of the spade determines the angle at which the head is held, which seems like an extremely convenient way to get the horse to hold his head the way you want him to. The spade bit is *not* a cruel bit, but like any other curb mouthpiece it must be handled correctly or it can cause the horse a good deal of discomfort.

Curb Bit Cheekpieces

A closer look at the action of curb bit *cheekpieces* shows that they can be classified on the basis of their leverage ratios. This ratio is determined by measuring from the mouthpiece to the rein loop and dividing this by the distance from the mouthpiece to the curb loop. Some short cheekpieces have leverage ratios higher than ones with long shanks. It should be remembered that these leverage ratios are concerned only with the multiplication of force, and it isn't at all unusual to find ratios which increase the applied force by a factor of three — a ten pound pull on the reins thus becomes a thirty pound force concentrated on four or five small points of control on the horses head.

The overall balance of the bit is influenced by the configuration of the cheekpieces. Extreme shapes should be avoided. The sweptback shape of the grazing bit is a good example of an extreme shape. It seems obvious that this bit can be carried comfortably by the horse only when he carries his nose fairly high, and his head extended. If the horse tucks his nose into an acceptable working position, the bit will fall forward and rock in the horse's mouth.

Weight seems to worry some individuals and there are many who believe that aluminum bits are automatically mild in their action. Such is not the case. Whether a bit is mild or severe depends upon its configuration, not on its weight. The fact is that the heavier steel bits seem to be more stable in the horse's mouth than do the light weight units.

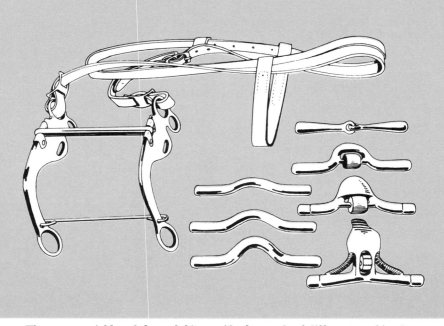

The many variables of the curb bit provide thousands of different combinations. Note mouthpieces pictured here: straight, low port, medium port, high port, snaffle, cricket, half-breed and spade.

The Curb Strap

An important part of the control achieved by the curb bit bridle is provided by the *curb strap*. There are many who look upon it as just another one of those straps which hold the bit in place. Such is not the case. The curb strap, or chain, applies a pressure to the curb groove which is an extremely sensitive area of control. Some horsemen believe that the curb strap exerts as much, if not more, control than does the curb bit mouthpiece, and point to the fact that one can achieve a more sensitive response by keeping the same mouthpiece and changing the curb strap to one of the more "severe" types. Of course, this also works the other way around. Probably only the horse knows for sure.

The fact does remain that the curb strap is a very important part of the curb mechanism and three basic types have been developed. The single link is probably the most popular. It provides the greatest control, but it is also the one that is most likely to rub and pinch. The double link provides a great deal of control, but is more mild

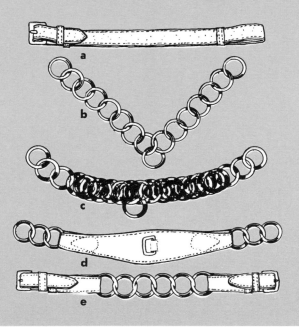

The curb strap is much more than just another strap that holds the bit in place. Change response by changing curb straps. (a) leather, (b) single chain, (c) double chain, (d) chain and strap, (e) strap and chain.

than the single link chain. The mildest of all is the plain leather strap. It presents a smooth surface, and is not near so likely to pinch or pull hairs, a fault common to the chain types. Whatever the type being used, it is advisable to remove all long hairs from the back of the chin and the curb groove. Your horse will be more comfortable for having done so.

Considering the many variables offered by the various components of the curb bit mechanism, one must recognize that it is a complex device. The many different mouthpieces times a vast array of cheekpieces gives one a total which could then be multiplied by a half dozen different curb straps, times about the same number of headstall variations. The result is literally thousands of different combinations, each of them just a little bit different from the others. Which one is best for your horse? Always strive for the mildest combination which works for the specific horse in question. It may take a little experimentation. All the expert advice you can get is also recommended. ∎

CHAPTER THIRTEEN

THE HACKAMORE

There are two basic types of *hackamores,* the *rawhide bosal* and the *mechanical hackamore.* The latter is sometimes referred to as a *hackamore bit.* Bosals are constructed with rawhide cores covered with braided rawhide. They come in various lengths and widths to fit all the various sizes and shapes of heads presented by different horses. Care should be used in the selection of the proper size and shape. The stiffer the bosal, the more control offered by this device.

The bosal curves around the horse's nose, passes down across the cheeks and joins under the jaws in a ball-like enlargement called the heel knot. Thick plaited horse hair reins (otherwise known as mecate reins) attach at the heel knot. This nosepiece (bosal) is attached to a regular headstall equipped with a browband.

The bosal works on the lower outside part of the jawbones, which has a thin covering of flesh and skin, and is thus quite sensitive. If the reins are pulled too harshly, the bosal can break through the skin — particularly if the bosal is quite stiff and heavy. As with all types of regular bits, care must be used.

The mechanical hackamore exerts pressure on two control areas, the nose and the curb groove. It is a little more sophisticated mechanism than the bosal in that it has a pair of metal cheekpieces to which the nosepiece attaches, and to which the curb strap is anchored. At the ends of the long shanks of the cheekpieces, regular reins attach in the same manner as with the curb bit. When the reins are pulled, the nosepiece and the curb strap is pressed into the sensitive control areas. There is a considerable leverage advantage provided by the long cheekpiece shanks which multiplies the force applied by the rider through the reins — something the horseman should remember in order to avoid causing his horse undue discomfort.

The degree of severity of the mechanical hackamore can be altered by choosing different nosepieces, and different curb straps. Wide, smooth-surfaced nosebands, such as that provided by the flat leather variety, are the most mild. Decreasing the width of the nosepiece, and constructing it out of a more roughly textured material increases

The bosal works on the lower outside part of the jawbones, which has a thin covering of skin and flesh and is therefore quite sensitive.

its severity. The braided rawhide type is probably the most popular but it is not as mild as most people think. If your horse shoots his nose up in the air when you pull on the reins, chances are that the nosepiece may be a little too severe. Choose one of the milder types. A sheepskin covering for the nosepiece provides the mildest control of all.

The laced nosepiece, which has a spring steel core, is the most severe of all, because the spring core keeps it in constant contact with the nose, and the least rein pressure will exert an increased pressure on the nose. This type is often chosen by horsemen for their performance horses which compete in barrel racing, pole bending and other gymkhana events.

Changing the response by altering the curb strap is done exactly as outlined in Chapter Twelve in conjunction with curb bits. The

The mechanical hackmore exerts pressure on two control areas, the nose and the curb groove. Severity varies with the nosepiece selected. (a) The flat, or sheepskin covered is the mildest. (b) The braided offers medium control. (c) The laced or solid leather nosepiece with a spring steel core is the most severe.

leather strap is the most mild and is certainly recommended over either of the chain types. If a more severe curb strap must be used, first try the double chain link, then move to the single chain — the most severe of all. ■